100
Writing Prompts
for High School

WALCH PUBLISHING

August Franza

SGS-SFI/COC-US09/5501

The classroom teacher may reproduce materials in this book for classroom use only.

The reproduction of any part for an entire school or school system is strictly prohibited.

No part of this publication may be transmitted, stored, or recorded in any form

without written permission from the publisher.

1   2   3   4   5   6   7   8   9   10

ISBN 0-8251-4993-2

Copyright © 1983, 1994, 2004
Walch Publishing
P.O. Box 658 • Portland, Maine 04104-0658
walch.com

Printed in the United States of America

Contents

To the Teacher

The rewards of Writing

Effective teacher direction, motivation, and encouragement are essential in cultivating successful writers in your English classes. Because most students will not volunteer to write essays, you need to do more than merely assign topics to be written about. You can generate enthusiasm for the rewards of writing by letting students know that you are genuinely interested in what they have to say. For their part, they must make every effort to be interesting writers. One of the best ways to accomplish this is for them to "write as they are," using their own experiences and perceptions. The composition activities in this book, designed for middle- and senior-high-school students of all abilities, invite students to use their sensory data, their memories, ideas, thoughts, opinions, and imaginations.

By the time students reach middle and high school, they have had a considerable amount of experience in life. They have lived for years in the vital environment of the family. They have gained and lost friends; they are finding out what truth, deceit, love, lies, and loyalty are all about; they have been in school for many years interacting with many adults and peers; they have favorite subjects which have stimulated their thinking and imagination; they are involved in and committed to sports; they have passionate hobbies; they are devoted to their friends; they are taking an active interest in the opposite sex; they are becoming more aware of their own individual selves at the same time that they are confronting the problems and demands of the larger society they were shielded from in childhood; they are beginning to wonder about some of the profound questions of life that adults grapple with; they are experiencing joys, problems, conflicts, and feelings of many kinds. All in all, they come into the English class with a large store of thoughts, feelings, observations, opinions, and experiences. They have to be encouraged to use these experiences in their writing. You might play upon this theme often, because if students lack anything, they lack the sure knowledge that their thoughts and experiences are of value.

While you are reinforcing the importance of experience in their writing, you might tell them about the realities of your situation—that you have 150 students in five classes and, as a result, you are a distracted audience in a very demanding job. Students should know that they will, in a sense, be vying for the attention of you, the reader, the audience of one. Which papers will you pick up and read first? Why? Because of their appearance? Because of the titles? Because of an interesting opening paragraph? Because of a certain stylistic effect? *Students have to realize that writing is not only self-expression, but communication directed at an audience.* Getting that audience's attention is an essential part of the communication process.

At the beginning of the school year, I tell my students that I will always try to create writing topics that interest me as well as them. In this way I will be curious to read what each student has to say. I tell them that arresting titles will determine which papers I read first, and also that the amount of interest generated by the opening sentence or paragraph will influence my feeling about what is to follow.

Essentially, I tell my students that there are two tasks in writing effectively. The first is to write from experience whenever possible, to trust one's sensory data, to have confidence in what one really knows. The second task is to be aware of the audience—in this case, the teacher who has a great deal to read and comparatively little time to do it in. This awareness should help motivate students to employ various techniques to ensure that the teacher will take an interest in the composition. Thus, on the one hand, students explore their worlds in order to find the materials for compositions. On the other hand, the students must project the material they choose from themselves to others in ways that will attract a reader's attention.

You, the curious teacher and reader, can make a considerable difference in the success of your writing program. You should be clear about what you want from students, create topics of interest for both you and your students, motivate them to be confident about using their hard-earned experience, and read the compositions as an interested party who will write a personal remark to each student, as well as correct and grade them.

It is my hope that the varied topics in this book will spark the process of writing and communication. The book is reproducible so that you can easily make photocopies of assignments and distribute them, thus saving the time required to write an assignment on the board and ensuring that each student has an accurate copy of the complete assignment.

—August Franza

The Life of an Artist

The life of an artist is very appealing because it permits individual expression. If you had your way, what kind of an artist would you like to be? Write an essay describing your possible achievements and what success would come of them.

_____

_____

_____

_____

_____

_____

_____

_____

_____

_____

_____

_____

_____

_____

_____

_____

_____

_____

_____

_____

_____

_____

Does Art Have Value?

"All art is quite useless," wrote Oscar Wilde. Do you think this statement is true? If so, then why do people go on making art? If you think the statement is **not** true, explain why. Whether you support or refute Wilde's statement, be sure to use specific examples in making your case.

_____

_____

_____

_____

_____

_____

_____

_____

_____

_____

_____

_____

_____

_____

_____

_____

_____

_____

_____

_____

_____

_____

_____

_____

The Art of Nature

In our highly industrialized and urbanized society, sometimes we forget about, ignore, or overlook the beauties of nature. But when we do have contact with nature, we often have a rich experience. Choose an example from your nature experiences and write an essay about it. Be descriptive so that the reader can also enjoy your discoveries.

_____

_____

_____

_____

_____

_____

_____

_____

_____

_____

_____

_____

_____

_____

_____

_____

_____

_____

_____

_____

_____

_____

The Art of Living

"When you begin the journey of life," said the wise man, "a mountain is a mountain and a river is a river. In the middle of the journey, a mountain is not a mountain and a river is not a river. But at the end of the journey, a mountain is a mountain and a river is a river."

Explain in an essay what the wise man means about searching and finding value in life. Be sure to distinguish between the first statement and the last.

_____

_____

_____

_____

_____

_____

_____

_____

_____

_____

_____

_____

_____

_____

_____

_____

_____

_____

_____

_____

_____

_____

Accident!

Describe in as much detail as you can recall an accident you witnessed or an accident you were involved in. You may write the account in one of two ways—on a journalistic level, or on a personal level. If you write on a journalistic level, be sure to include the five W's: who, what, when, where, and why.

_____

_____

_____

_____

_____

_____

_____

_____

_____

_____

_____

_____

_____

_____

_____

_____

_____

_____

_____

_____

_____

Big Wheels

Who or what are the "big wheels" in your life? What do you think of them? Are you one of them? Do they get special attention and special consideration? Are you envious of them? Do you have strong positive or negative feelings about them? Organize your thoughts and feelings and write an essay called "Big Wheels."

_____

_____

_____

_____

_____

_____

_____

_____

_____

_____

_____

_____

_____

_____

_____

_____

_____

_____

_____

_____

_____

_____

_____

The Person at the Wheel

The person at the wheel is a tough leader. He knows what he's doing and he can handle adversity. Describe a leader you know. It may be your father, mother, teacher, coach, or even the president of the United States! Describe what she or he does to deserve the name of leader.

_____

_____

_____

_____

_____

_____

_____

_____

_____

_____

_____

_____

_____

_____

_____

_____

_____

_____

_____

_____

_____

_____

_____

Are Ceremonies Necessary?

Shakespeare said that true friendship needs no ceremonies. Is this true? Why? Why not? In an essay, defend or attack Shakespeare's observation.

_____

_____

_____

_____

_____

_____

_____

_____

_____

_____

_____

_____

_____

_____

_____

_____

_____

_____

_____

_____

_____

_____

_____

_____

Are Ceremonies a Crutch?

Someone has said that ceremonies were devised to make faint deeds attractive. That is, under normal circumstances there is really nothing to applaud or praise. But surround a slight deed with ceremony and it will look good. Support or reject this observation using specific experiences of your own.

_____

_____

_____

_____

_____

_____

_____

_____

_____

_____

_____

_____

_____

_____

_____

_____

_____

_____

_____

_____

_____

_____

_____

A Family Ceremony

Every family has its own unique ceremonies that, possibly, no other family would understand. Does your family have one? Do you know of a family with such a ceremony? Describe it. When did it start?

_____

_____

_____

_____

_____

_____

_____

_____

_____

_____

_____

_____

_____

_____

_____

_____

_____

_____

_____

_____

_____

_____

_____

_____

A Day in the City

Describe an eventful day you spent in a city. Maybe you went with friends, with your parents, or with a class. Where did you go? What did you see? What did you do? How tired did you get? What were your feelings about the trip?

_____

_____

_____

_____

_____

_____

_____

_____

_____

_____

_____

_____

_____

_____

_____

_____

_____

_____

_____

_____

_____

_____

A City of the Future

Create a city of the future. Give it a name and tell us where it will be. What will it look like? What will take place in your city? How will it be different from twenty-first century cities?

_____

_____

_____

_____

_____

_____

_____

_____

_____

_____

_____

_____

_____

_____

_____

_____

_____

_____

_____

_____

_____

_____

A Special Place
in the Country

In George Orwell's *1984*, Winston Smith dreams of "the Golden Country," a place in the country, far away from the city, with a clear, slow-moving stream, covered by a canopy of willow trees. What is your special place in the country? Describe it in detail. Where is it? At what time of the year do you like it the best? The place can be real or a part of your imagination.

_____

_____

_____

_____

_____

_____

_____

_____

_____

_____

_____

_____

_____

_____

_____

_____

_____

_____

_____

_____

_____

Night in the City

Let your imagination go and describe a night in the city. If you are from the city, describe an actual night in the city as you know it. If you are not from the city, describe a night as you imagine it. In either case, be dramatic, and use vivid language.

_____

_____

_____

_____

_____

_____

_____

_____

_____

_____

_____

_____

_____

_____

_____

_____

_____

_____

_____

_____

_____

_____

The Most Important Lesson

What's the most important lesson you've ever learned at school? Was it something from a book, a film, a teacher, a schoolmate? In an essay, explain the circumstances, what you found out, and how your discovery has influenced you.

_____

_____

_____

_____

_____

_____

_____

_____

_____

_____

_____

_____

_____

_____

_____

_____

_____

_____

_____

_____

_____

_____

_____

_____

_____

Dropping Out

Do you regard dropping out of school as a catastrophe? Or do you believe it's something every student has a right to do? Take a position and support your point of view.

_____

_____

_____

_____

_____

_____

_____

_____

_____

_____

_____

_____

_____

_____

_____

_____

_____

_____

_____

_____

_____

_____

_____

Revolution in English

Do you agree with George Bernard Shaw that English spelling ought to be simplified? After all, eighty percent of our words are not spelled the way they sound! That's why we have so many spelling tests and spelling bees. Few other languages need them because their words are spelled the way they sound. Shaw said English is so crazy that you can spell the word *fish* this way: *ghoti*. How? The *f* sound as in *tough*, the *i* as in *women*, the *sh* as in *nation*. Write an editorial demanding simplification of spelling and give your reasons why.

_____
_____
_____
_____
_____
_____
_____
_____
_____
_____
_____
_____
_____
_____
_____
_____
_____
_____
_____
_____
_____

Safety in School

How safe do you feel in school? Have you had any experiences that shake your ease and confidence? Describe them. Do you have any proposals for making your school safer? State them at the conclusion of your essay in a persuasive way.

_____

_____

_____

_____

_____

_____

_____

_____

_____

_____

_____

_____

_____

_____

_____

_____

_____

_____

_____

_____

_____

_____

_____

_____

Condoms in School

The fear of the spread of STD's has caused some school districts in the United States to make condoms available to students. Do you think this is a good or bad idea? Examine your position and then express it with conviction.

_____

_____

_____

_____

_____

_____

_____

_____

_____

_____

_____

_____

_____

_____

_____

_____

_____

_____

_____

_____

_____

_____

_____

_____

_____

Food, Food, Wonderful Food

You have your favorite foods, and you know how good food tastes when you're famished. Imagine a waiter has appeared at your side right now. Describe the perfect meal that you are about to order.

_____

_____

_____

_____

_____

_____

_____

_____

_____

_____

_____

_____

_____

_____

_____

_____

_____

_____

_____

_____

Another Kind of Food

A wise man said, "If you have but two pennies left, buy bread with one and a rose with the other." In an essay, explain the wise man's philosophy.

_____

_____

_____

_____

_____

_____

_____

_____

_____

_____

_____

_____

_____

_____

_____

_____

_____

_____

_____

_____

_____

_____

_____

_____

_____

_____

_____

Health Food

"Health Food" is a misnomer, isn't it? After all, all food contributes to health. Nevertheless, the term "health food" means to suggest organically grown foods (no pesticides), low-fat and low-sodium foods, avoidance of red meat (replacing it with tofu products), and use of vitamin supplements. Health food is also quite a bit more expensive. Are you a health food fan or critic? Take a position and fire away.

_____
_____
_____
_____
_____
_____
_____
_____
_____
_____
_____
_____
_____
_____
_____
_____
_____
_____
_____
_____
_____
_____
_____

Advice for Mother (or Father)

Whether he or she likes it or not, or wants to hear it or not, you have some advice to give to your father or mother. Write a letter giving that advice, the reasons why you are giving the advice, and the results to be expected if the advice is taken.

_____

_____

_____

_____

_____

_____

_____

_____

_____

_____

_____

_____

_____

_____

_____

_____

_____

_____

_____

_____

_____

_____

_____

_____

Changes

Find a picture of yourself and your family that's more than ten years old. Study each person in the picture. Now write a reflective essay called "Who I Was; Who I Am Now."

_____

_____

_____

_____

_____

_____

_____

_____

_____

_____

_____

_____

_____

_____

_____

_____

_____

_____

_____

_____

_____

_____

My Favorite TV Family

Which family on TV is your favorite? Why? In an essay, describe your favorite family, giving the characteristics of each member and why each member is so interesting or appealing to you. (You might wish to replace "TV" with "movie" family or a family depicted in a novel.)

_____

_____

_____

_____

_____

_____

_____

_____

_____

_____

_____

_____

_____

_____

_____

_____

_____

_____

_____

_____

_____

_____

_____

Unwed Mothers

There's a new mode of motherhood—unmarried women are deciding to have babies rather than waiting, possibly too long, for a satisfactory spouse. What is your opinion of these decisions?

_____

_____

_____

_____

_____

_____

_____

_____

_____

_____

_____

_____

_____

_____

_____

_____

_____

_____

_____

_____

_____

_____

_____

Death Penalty

There are many people who believe in the death penalty. They think the death penalty should be imposed for crimes such as murder and treason. Their theory is that a fear of death will stop people from committing these crimes. Therefore, the death penalty is a very useful measure. Support, reject, or qualify this argument. In doing so, develop your own thoughts beyond what's stated here.

_____

_____

_____

_____

_____

_____

_____

_____

_____

_____

_____

_____

_____

_____

_____

_____

_____

_____

_____

_____

A Glass Dictionary

"The world is a glass dictionary," wrote Ralph Waldo Emerson. What does he mean by that remark? Is he right? Or do you think the world is an opaque dictionary? Take a position and support your views with examples drawn from your experience.

_____

_____

_____

_____

_____

_____

_____

_____

_____

_____

_____

_____

_____

_____

_____

_____

_____

_____

_____

_____

_____

_____

My Society

"Ours is a self-indulgent, self-centered society." So say some of our critics. Do you agree or disagree? Whichever position you take, be specific in pointing out a variety of instances and experiences that support your point of view.

_____

_____

_____

_____

_____

_____

_____

_____

_____

_____

_____

_____

_____

_____

_____

_____

_____

_____

_____

_____

_____

_____

_____

Gun Control

Should there be stricter gun-control laws? Write, if you can, from your own experience. If not, review the arguments and state your position forcefully.

_____

_____

_____

_____

_____

_____

_____

_____

_____

_____

_____

_____

_____

_____

_____

_____

_____

_____

_____

_____

_____

_____

_____

_____

_____

Drunk Driving

Describe the efforts—or lack of efforts—of your school and community regarding the issue of driving under the influence of alcohol or drugs.

_____

_____

_____

_____

_____

_____

_____

_____

_____

_____

_____

_____

_____

_____

_____

_____

_____

_____

_____

_____

_____

_____

_____

_____

My Hobby

There are few things as satisfying as a hobby. Describe yours. Describe it and put the pleasure of your feelings into the essay so that the reader can appreciate your hobby almost as much as you do.

_____

_____

_____

_____

_____

_____

_____

_____

_____

_____

_____

_____

_____

_____

_____

_____

_____

_____

_____

_____

_____

_____

_____

Winter/Summer Recreation

In the parts of the country where the weather changes dramatically, it's necessary to have both winter and summer recreation. In other parts of the country, seasonal weather doesn't change much at all. Contrast your form of winter and summer recreation.

_____

_____

_____

_____

_____

_____

_____

_____

_____

_____

_____

_____

_____

_____

_____

_____

_____

_____

_____

_____

_____

_____

_____

Spending Money

One of the surest tests of a person's real desires is to find out what he or she thinks is worthwhile to spend money on. Compare two people's spending habits (perhaps your own). What do these habits reveal about that person?

_____

_____

_____

_____

_____

_____

_____

_____

_____

_____

_____

_____

_____

_____

_____

_____

_____

_____

_____

_____

_____

_____

_____

_____

_____

Is Life Just a Game?

Many people have said, after living a long time, that life is just a game. They mean that it shouldn't be taken seriously. People are thrust into situations and they play their roles as best they can. They didn't pick their roles, so why take them seriously? Some win, some lose, and there's usually another game to play in another season. Do you agree? If you do, support the view with evidence from your experience. If you don't, criticize the view and indicate the correct attitude, as far as you are concerned.

_____

_____

_____

_____

_____

_____

_____

_____

_____

_____

_____

_____

_____

_____

_____

_____

_____

_____

_____

_____

_____

_____

_____

A Work-Free Birthday?

Do you think you are entitled to have your birthday off from work or school without being penalized for it? Take a position and justify it in a letter to the editor in your local paper.

_____

_____

_____

_____

_____

_____

_____

_____

_____

_____

_____

_____

_____

_____

_____

_____

_____

_____

_____

_____

_____

_____

_____

_____

_____

New Year's Eve and Nothing to Do!

What's more disturbing than having nothing to do on New Year's Eve? Describe the feelings of a person who's alone on New Year's Eve. You may want to put the thoughts and feelings in the form of a journal entry.

_____

_____

_____

_____

_____

_____

_____

_____

_____

_____

_____

_____

_____

_____

_____

_____

_____

_____

_____

_____

_____

_____

More Holidays!

You may be of the opinion that there are not enough holidays in the school year. So invent some! Make up three new holidays which are so important that school has to be closed a week for each holiday. How about a World Series Holiday or a Superbowl Holiday that gives you the week off? Justify your holiday with strong arguments.

_____

_____

_____

_____

_____

_____

_____

_____

_____

_____

_____

_____

_____

_____

_____

_____

_____

_____

_____

_____

_____

_____

A Character I'll Remember

Describe a character you have recently met in your reading. Why is this character memorable? What are his or her outstanding traits? What problem(s) has the character overcome?

_____

_____

_____

_____

_____

_____

_____

_____

_____

_____

_____

_____

_____

_____

_____

_____

_____

_____

_____

_____

_____

_____

_____

Banning Books

Do you believe certain books should be banned? After all, words are very influential, and people, especially the young, are very impressionable. Shouldn't they be protected? Take a definite position, either yes or no, and explain your position fully and clearly.

_____

_____

_____

_____

_____

_____

_____

_____

_____

_____

_____

_____

_____

_____

_____

_____

_____

_____

_____

_____

_____

_____

Rereading a Book

Most of us read books only once. But there are few books in our lives that we love going back to and rereading. Discuss such a literary experience of yours and indicate why you reread the book.

_____

_____

_____

_____

_____

_____

_____

_____

_____

_____

_____

_____

_____

_____

_____

_____

_____

_____

_____

_____

_____

_____

_____

Is Literature Life?

Some writers and critics believe that readers can learn a great deal about life through literature. Other writers and critics, such as Oscar Wilde and Vladimir Nabokov, believe that literature is a toy, a game, and has nothing to offer but pleasure. Which view do you support? Explain why you support it.

_____

_____

_____

_____

_____

_____

_____

_____

_____

_____

_____

_____

_____

_____

_____

_____

_____

_____

_____

_____

_____

_____

_____

Defending Rap and Hip-Hop

Rap and hip-hop, some critics say, represent deterioration in the values of American culture. The crude thumping and unvarying beat are symptoms of a numbness that tunes listeners out. Do you agree or disagree? Using arguments that you, yourself, believe, defend your position.

_____

_____

_____

_____

_____

_____

_____

_____

_____

_____

_____

_____

_____

_____

_____

_____

_____

_____

_____

_____

_____

_____

_____

Music of Sounds

Keep a record of the sounds you hear in the course of a day. The purpose is to pay attention to the environment you live in every day. Then write an essay describing the sounds you have heard and recorded, no matter how ugly, trivial, or ordinary you may think they are. Try to make your readers as aware of the sounds as you are.

_____

_____

_____

_____

_____

_____

_____

_____

_____

_____

_____

_____

_____

_____

_____

_____

_____

_____

_____

_____

_____

_____

Life Without Music

The philosopher Nietzsche said that without music, life is a mistake. Do you agree or disagree? Fully or partially? Take a position, based on your own experience. Is life without music a mistake?

_____

_____

_____

_____

_____

_____

_____

_____

_____

_____

_____

_____

_____

_____

_____

_____

_____

_____

_____

_____

_____

_____

_____

_____

_____

Universal Language?

It's often said that music is a universal language. But is it really? People often despise the other fellow's music. So what's so universal about it? Examine this puzzle in a meditative essay.

_____

_____

_____

_____

_____

_____

_____

_____

_____

_____

_____

_____

_____

_____

_____

_____

_____

_____

_____

_____

_____

_____

_____

Writing a Script

Invent a story and write the script for a three-minute movie you could make. It must be a simple story with a beginning, a middle, an end, and a few characters. The script must describe the camera shots and their length. Remember that you have only 180 seconds to work with.

_____

_____

_____

_____

_____

_____

_____

_____

_____

_____

_____

_____

_____

_____

_____

_____

_____

_____

_____

_____

A Miserable Time at the Movies

Conditions in the movie theater you are sitting in can be so distracting that you end up having a miserable time. Describe such an experience. There may have been cockroaches in the popcorn, a fight in the crowd, or a damaged print of the film projected on the screen.

_____

_____

_____

_____

_____

_____

_____

_____

_____

_____

_____

_____

_____

_____

_____

_____

_____

_____

_____

_____

_____

If I Were a Movie Star...

Imagine your life as a movie star. Give yourself a movie name and describe in your journal how your life goes from day to day.

_____

_____

_____

_____

_____

_____

_____

_____

_____

_____

_____

_____

_____

_____

_____

_____

_____

_____

_____

_____

_____

_____

_____

_____

_____

Smile, These Are the Best Years of Your Life

Often, teenagers are told that their teen years are the best years of their lives. They are usually told this when the expression on their face or their behavior says just the opposite. Based on your own experience, support or reject this observation.

_____

_____

_____

_____

_____

_____

_____

_____

_____

_____

_____

_____

_____

_____

_____

_____

_____

_____

_____

_____

_____

_____

A New Rule

"The failure of existing rules," a philosopher wrote, "is the prelude to a search for new ones." Select one rule in your home or in your school that you think has failed, and show by examples that it is unworkable. Then, provide a new rule or procedure that you feel will work. Describe fully why you think it's a better rule than the one it will replace.

_____

_____

_____

_____

_____

_____

_____

_____

_____

_____

_____

_____

_____

_____

_____

_____

_____

_____

_____

_____

_____

_____

_____

A Face

George Orwell wrote that, by the age of fifty, each of us has the face he or she deserves. This means that our life's experience leave their marks on the surface of our skin. They also influence the muscle and bone structure. Therefore, a person's face may describe the kind of life he or she has led. Find a good, clear photo of an adult face and imagine the experiences that have made the face what it is today.

_____

_____

_____

_____

_____

_____

_____

_____

_____

_____

_____

_____

_____

_____

_____

_____

_____

_____

_____

_____

Clothes Make the Man
(or Woman)

What a person wears, whether by choice or necessity, reveals a great deal about him or her. Some people regard clothing as a symbol of status, wealth, or personal taste. Others think that dress is less important. How do you feel about it? Think of two or more individuals you know, and discuss in an essay what their clothing tells you about each one's personality, character, or circumstances.

_____

_____

_____

_____

_____

_____

_____

_____

_____

_____

_____

_____

_____

_____

_____

_____

_____

_____

_____

_____

_____

_____

_____

_____

A Morning It Didn't Pay to Get Out of Bed

Who can't relate to this topic? We have a sixth sense about these matters. You wake warily. You dress cautiously. You go about your business looking over your shoulder. Then when "it" happens, you know that for sure it didn't pay to get out of bed. Describe such a day in your life.

_____

_____

_____

_____

_____

_____

_____

_____

_____

_____

_____

_____

_____

_____

_____

_____

_____

_____

_____

_____

_____

_____

A Short Life

You may know of a short life—someone that has died young. Describe this person and the effect of his or her death on you, as well as others.

_____

_____

_____

_____

_____

_____

_____

_____

_____

_____

_____

_____

_____

_____

_____

_____

_____

_____

_____

_____

_____

_____

_____

_____

_____

_____

A Hero

Who is your personal hero? Is he or she a sports figure, someone you know personally, a star in the movies or on TV? Describe your hero in detail.

_____

_____

_____

_____

_____

_____

_____

_____

_____

_____

_____

_____

_____

_____

_____

_____

_____

_____

_____

_____

_____

_____

_____

_____

_____

What's a Flag?

What's a flag? What does it stand for? What emotions does it evoke? You may wish to recall incidents in your life where a flag was involved—a parade, a celebration, a holiday, or a ceremony. Try to bring this moment to life.

_____

_____

_____

_____

_____

_____

_____

_____

_____

_____

_____

_____

_____

_____

_____

_____

_____

_____

_____

_____

_____

_____

_____

Commencement Address

For this year's commencement address at your high school, you have been asked to make a speech. The Board of Education wants to hear your philosophy of education. Write the speech you wish to deliver.

_____

_____

_____

_____

_____

_____

_____

_____

_____

_____

_____

_____

_____

_____

_____

_____

_____

_____

_____

_____

_____

_____

_____

_____

_____

_____

_____

Animal Experimentation: Yes or No?

Should the use of animals in research and teaching be stopped, or should persons engaged in experimentation, for the benefit of humankind, have the right to use animals? Take a position. Support your answer. Suggest your view of how animals should be used.

_____

_____

_____

_____

_____

_____

_____

_____

_____

_____

_____

_____

_____

_____

_____

_____

_____

_____

_____

_____

_____

Simplify, Simplify

Henry David Thoreau believed that in order to live well, we must reduce the number of material goods we have. Otherwise, these things begin to dominate us. Take a position about this in regard to your life. Should you simplify your life? What would you give up? Or do you think that in our day and age you should increase what you own, not limit it?

_____

_____

_____

_____

_____

_____

_____

_____

_____

_____

_____

_____

_____

_____

_____

_____

_____

_____

_____

_____

_____

_____

_____

Free Speech

How important, in your mind, is the First Amendment to the Constitution? Is it essential to American life, or could we live without it?

_____

_____

_____

_____

_____

_____

_____

_____

_____

_____

_____

_____

_____

_____

_____

_____

_____

_____

_____

_____

_____

_____

_____

_____

_____

Madam President

A woman for president! Describe in an editorial why this is a necessary step in American politics. What effects will it have?

_____

_____

_____

_____

_____

_____

_____

_____

_____

_____

_____

_____

_____

_____

_____

_____

_____

_____

_____

_____

_____

_____

_____

_____

_____

Abortion

The issue of abortion, like no other, pits people against one another because it touches their core beliefs. And we know that core beliefs do not change with the times. What is your position on abortion?

_____

_____

_____

_____

_____

_____

_____

_____

_____

_____

_____

_____

_____

_____

_____

_____

_____

_____

_____

_____

_____

_____

_____

_____

Stranded!

All of us, at one time or another, has been left stranded. Or we've felt stranded—alone and abandoned. Describe such an experience in your life, when you were "up the creek without a paddle" and were left to your own devices. What happened and what did you learn?

_____

_____

_____

_____

_____

_____

_____

_____

_____

_____

_____

_____

_____

_____

_____

_____

_____

_____

_____

_____

_____

_____

The Obstacle

Everybody faces obstacles in life. They may be physical, social, or even psychological. Often they are financial. Describe in detail an obstacle that you are facing, and explain how you hope to overcome it. Perhaps you may have already faced the problem. Then tell us how you overcame it or failed to overcome it.

_____

_____

_____

_____

_____

_____

_____

_____

_____

_____

_____

_____

_____

_____

_____

_____

_____

_____

_____

_____

_____

_____

A Deadly Fear

What is your greatest fear, and how did it originate? Write a letter to a friend describing your fear. How does it limit you? Have you tried to overcome it? Do you expect to be rid of it soon?

_____

_____

_____

_____

_____

_____

_____

_____

_____

_____

_____

_____

_____

_____

_____

_____

_____

_____

_____

_____

_____

_____

_____

The Biggest Problem
of Our Time

What, in your opinion, is the biggest problem of our time? In an essay, identify this problem and explain in detail why it is such a gigantic problem.

_____

_____

_____

_____

_____

_____

_____

_____

_____

_____

_____

_____

_____

_____

_____

_____

_____

_____

_____

_____

_____

_____

_____

_____

A Problem at School

Consider a problem at school that you find upsetting and distressing.
Describe the problem fully. What do you think can be done to solve it?

_____

_____

_____

_____

_____

_____

_____

_____

_____

_____

_____

_____

_____

_____

_____

_____

_____

_____

_____

_____

_____

_____

_____

_____

Lottery

Suppose you bought a lottery ticket and won a million dollars? What will you do with that money, earned by chance? Will you indulge yourself? Will you share it? Will you invest it? Will you give it to the poor?

_____

_____

_____

_____

_____

_____

_____

_____

_____

_____

_____

_____

_____

_____

_____

_____

_____

_____

_____

_____

_____

_____

_____

_____

Unlimited Powers!

Imagine you have been granted one week of unlimited powers and can exercise these powers only once. What would you choose to do? Why would you choose to do it? Show what the varied consequences will be.

_____

_____

_____

_____

_____

_____

_____

_____

_____

_____

_____

_____

_____

_____

_____

_____

_____

_____

_____

_____

_____

_____

_____

_____

_____

I Am Grimaldi

Once there was a man who was very sad and depressed. He was near suicide. The doctor gave him only one suggestion; he was sure it would help the man. He told the man to go and see the great clown Grimaldi. The man looked at the doctor and said, "I am Grimaldi."

Continue this story. In a dialogue form, tell the reader what conversation follows this episode. What can the doctor possibly say? What will Grimaldi reveal?

_____

_____

_____

_____

_____

_____

_____

_____

_____

_____

_____

_____

_____

_____

_____

_____

_____

_____

_____

_____

_____

_____

Dinnertime Conversation

Imagine you are married and have a family of teenagers. One evening, you, your spouse, and your children sit down to dinner. During the course of it, your 18-year-old daughter tells you that she is quitting college, moving out of the house, and going to live in the city to look for a career. Write a one-scene play that reveals everybody's reactions and suggestions. Reveal, too, how dinner turns out.

_____

_____

_____

_____

_____

_____

_____

_____

_____

_____

_____

_____

_____

_____

_____

_____

_____

_____

_____

_____

_____

_____

The Day It Rained Colors

They forecast rain, but you didn't expect this! You look out your window and it's raining all the colors of the spectrum. A further look and you see the colors are sticking to people and to objects. Describe how the world changed the day it rained colors. Was the change temporary or permanent? Write a story about the events and make sure it shimmers with color.

_____

_____

_____

_____

_____

_____

_____

_____

_____

_____

_____

_____

_____

_____

_____

_____

_____

_____

_____

_____

_____

_____

_____

Saying Good-bye

No one likes to say good-bye, but saying it is sometimes inevitable. Write an essay about a person to whom you had to say good-bye. Who is this person? What were the circumstances that caused you to part? How did you feel? What were your thoughts?

_____

_____

_____

_____

_____

_____

_____

_____

_____

_____

_____

_____

_____

_____

_____

_____

_____

_____

_____

_____

_____

_____

_____

_____

_____

Partying!

Many teenagers love partying. Some do not. Describe this social experience from your own point of view. What does partying mean to you?

_____

_____

_____

_____

_____

_____

_____

_____

_____

_____

_____

_____

_____

_____

_____

_____

_____

_____

_____

_____

_____

_____

_____

_____

_____

_____

_____

Fictional But Real

Describe a relationship between two people in a novel or play you have read or seen. This relationship may be positive and loving or neurotic and defeating. Describe this relationship in detail and explain why it attracts you.

_____

_____

_____

_____

_____

_____

_____

_____

_____

_____

_____

_____

_____

_____

_____

_____

_____

_____

_____

_____

_____

_____

A Perfect Relationship

You may know two people whom you think have a perfect relationship, or as perfect a relationship as is humanly possible. Who are those people? Describe their relationship as you see it.

_____

_____

_____

_____

_____

_____

_____

_____

_____

_____

_____

_____

_____

_____

_____

_____

_____

_____

_____

_____

_____

_____

_____

_____

_____

_____

The Clothes I'd Like to Wear—But Don't Dare!

Describe the clothes, and the occasion on which you would wear them, if you could unleash your inhibitions (or others' inhibitions). Tell why you would like to do this.

_____

_____

_____

_____

_____

_____

_____

_____

_____

_____

_____

_____

_____

_____

_____

_____

_____

_____

_____

_____

_____

_____

Self-Expression in My House

What's self-expression like in your house? Do people say what has to be said, no holds barred? Is everybody restrained and genteel? Is there a happy medium? Describe what it's like in your house.

_____

_____

_____

_____

_____

_____

_____

_____

_____

_____

_____

_____

_____

_____

_____

_____

_____

_____

_____

_____

_____

Talking Back

Choose a man or woman in history to whom you'd like to say a lot. Maybe you'd like to tell Napoleon off, or Hitler. Maybe you'd like to give Joan of Arc some practical advice, or maybe Eve in the Garden. Choose a historical figure, sit him or her down, and start talking!

_____

_____

_____

_____

_____

_____

_____

_____

_____

_____

_____

_____

_____

_____

_____

_____

_____

_____

_____

_____

_____

_____

Playing the Game

According to some commentators, winning should not be the paramount goal in sports competition. The paramount goals should be enjoyment, physical expression, and dedication. Which goal is paramount for you? Write an essay defending your position.

_____

_____

_____

_____

_____

_____

_____

_____

_____

_____

_____

_____

_____

_____

_____

_____

_____

_____

_____

_____

_____

A Game That Taught Me a Lesson

Sports, we are often told, are a lot like life; there's much to be learned about life by playing sports. Did you ever play a game in which the experience and outcome taught you an important lesson? Write about your experience and the lesson that you learned.

_____

_____

_____

_____

_____

_____

_____

_____

_____

_____

_____

_____

_____

_____

_____

_____

_____

_____

_____

_____

_____

_____

No More Sports!

Suppose all interscholastic sports had to be dropped for economic reasons. While you would be able to play these sports during gym period, all competition between schools would be at an end. Would this be a good or bad decision? What effect would it have on your education? Would you approve or disapprove of the decision?

_____

_____

_____

_____

_____

_____

_____

_____

_____

_____

_____

_____

_____

_____

_____

_____

_____

_____

_____

_____

_____

_____

Players' Pay

Are today's professional players of sports paid too much? Are they worth the money they get? Take a position and let go!

_____

_____

_____

_____

_____

_____

_____

_____

_____

_____

_____

_____

_____

_____

_____

_____

_____

_____

_____

_____

_____

_____

_____

_____

Child-Free

A happily married couple decides to have no children. Some of the couple's reasons are global overcrowding, impending ecological crises, possible nuclear accidents and wars, and the desire to pursue careers without interruption. Write an essay in which you agree or disagree with this couple's decision. Provide specific reasons for your opinions.

_____

_____

_____

_____

_____

_____

_____

_____

_____

_____

_____

_____

_____

_____

_____

_____

_____

_____

_____

_____

_____

_____

_____

_____

_____

Fear of the Future

Do you have any fears of the future? Think about different reasons for this fear. Write a monologue giving all the reasons and the feelings behind them.

_____

_____

_____

_____

_____

_____

_____

_____

_____

_____

_____

_____

_____

_____

_____

_____

_____

_____

_____

_____

_____

_____

_____

_____

A New Human Being?

Will the future bring a new kind of man and woman? Utopian writers have often conceived of an improved human being in an improved world. Anti-utopian writers often show human beings at their worst. Write a utopian story of your own. Make a decision before you write whether the people of the future are going to be better than we are or worse. Give your utopia or anti-utopia a name.

_____

_____

_____

_____

_____

_____

_____

_____

_____

_____

_____

_____

_____

_____

_____

_____

_____

_____

_____

_____

_____

_____

_____

_____

_____

Past Perfect or
Past Forgotten?

One philosopher said "You can never plan the future by the past." Another said that if you don't pay attention to the past, you will be doomed to relive all the same mistakes. Which philosopher do you agree with? What philosophy are you going to employ in your life?

_____

_____

_____

_____

_____

_____

_____

_____

_____

_____

_____

_____

_____

_____

_____

_____

_____

_____

_____

_____

_____

_____

A TV Show of My Own

You've been given an opportunity to propose a TV show of your own making, so here's your big chance. Write a memo to the president of a major network outlining your show. Will it be a sitcom, a sports show, a talk show, a variety show? Will it be an hour or a half-hour show? Live or taped?

_____

_____

_____

_____

_____

_____

_____

_____

_____

_____

_____

_____

_____

_____

_____

_____

_____

_____

_____

_____

_____

_____

_____

Things I've Learned from TV

There is a theory that says that TV is the real educator in the lives of the young. Do you agree? What have you learned from TV that you consider substantial and important?

_____

_____

_____

_____

_____

_____

_____

_____

_____

_____

_____

_____

_____

_____

_____

_____

_____

_____

_____

_____

_____

_____

A New TV Commercial

Invent a new product. Write all the copy that will be necessary for a one-minute commercial. Give your product a name.

_____

_____

_____

_____

_____

_____

_____

_____

_____

_____

_____

_____

_____

_____

_____

_____

_____

_____

_____

_____

_____

_____

_____

_____

_____

Is TV Responsible for the Rise in Violence?

Take a stand on this controversial question, based on your own experience watching TV. Write a letter to your congressperson and give him or her your point-blank view of this question. Defend your position to him or her.

_____

_____

_____

_____

_____

_____

_____

_____

_____

_____

_____

_____

_____

_____

_____

_____

_____

_____

_____

_____

_____

_____

_____

_____

The Day TV Died

    Write a story about one person's reactions to the banning of TV by government edict. "On January 1, 20__, all TV sets were turned off" could be your opening line. What is this person's reaction? What does he or she do about it?

_____

_____

_____

_____

_____

_____

_____

_____

_____

_____

_____

_____

_____

_____

_____

_____

_____

_____

_____

_____

_____

_____

_____

_____

A Long-Distance Voyage

All of us can be long-distance voyagers—in our minds and imaginations. All we have to do is start daydreaming, and the most amazing experiences can occur. We can travel anywhere and go first-class, too. With this in mind, take such a voyage to the stars or deep into the past. Describe what you find in detail.

_____

_____

_____

_____

_____

_____

_____

_____

_____

_____

_____

_____

_____

_____

_____

_____

_____

_____

_____

_____

_____

_____

Getting There Is All the Fun

Robert Louis Stevenson wrote, "To travel hopefully is better than to arrive." He meant that the journey is more rewarding than the reaching of the destination, no matter how rewarding that may be. Can you see his point? Has there been a time in your life when the journey was more rewarding than the arrival, when preparation for an event turned out to be more fulfilling than the event itself? Tell your story.

_____

_____

_____

_____

_____

_____

_____

_____

_____

_____

_____

_____

_____

_____

_____

_____

_____

_____

_____

_____

_____

_____

Travel Is So Broadening

"Travel is broadening" is an old cliché. But it can also be a true statement. Has it been your experience? Tell of a trip you've taken in which you've learned a great deal about other people and other cultures, or explain why you would like to travel.

_____

_____

_____

_____

_____

_____

_____

_____

_____

_____

_____

_____

_____

_____

_____

_____

_____

_____

_____

_____

_____

_____

Working for Others or Myself?

Do you want to work for someone else or be self-employed? Why do you have this particular preference? Has anyone influenced you in regard to this preference?

_____

_____

_____

_____

_____

_____

_____

_____

_____

_____

_____

_____

_____

_____

_____

_____

_____

_____

_____

_____

_____

_____

_____

_____

_____

I Like Work . . .

"I like work," says the popular proverb. "It fascinates me. I can sit and look at it for hours." Do you agree that it's far more fun to relax than to work? Describe the various ways you have of getting out of work. A humorous approach might be useful in this essay.

_____

_____

_____

_____

_____

_____

_____

_____

_____

_____

_____

_____

_____

_____

_____

_____

_____

_____

_____

_____

_____

_____

Love Plus Work

Sigmund Freud wrote that love plus work equals happiness. Do you agree with this formula, or do you have a better one? Freud meant, quite simply, that having someone to love and having meaningful work would add up to happiness.

_____

_____

_____

_____

_____

_____

_____

_____

_____

_____

_____

_____

_____

_____

_____

_____

_____

_____

_____

_____

_____

Success for Me

How much success will make you happy? What would you like to be successful at? When will you know that you are a success? Under what circumstances? In an essay, pinpoint your answers to these questions.

_____

_____

_____

_____

_____

_____

_____

_____

_____

_____

_____

_____

_____

_____

_____

_____

_____

_____

_____

_____

_____

_____

Share Your Bright Ideas

We want to hear from you!

Your name_____Date_____

School name_____

School address_____

City _____State _____Zip_____Phone number (_____)_____

Grade level(s) taught_____Subject area(s) taught_____

Where did you purchase this publication?_____

In what month do you purchase a majority of your supplements?_____

What moneys were used to purchase this product?

____School supplemental budget   ____Federal/state funding   ____Personal

Please "grade" this Walch publication in the following areas:

Quality of service you received when purchasing .... A   B   C   D

Ease of use.. A   B   C   D

Quality of content.. A   B   C   D

Page layout .... A   B   C   D

Organization of material .... A   B   C   D

Suitability for grade level .... A   B   C   D

Instructional value.. A   B   C   D

COMMENTS:_____

_____

What specific supplemental materials would help you meet your current—or future—instructional needs?

_____

Have you used other Walch publications? If so, which ones?_____

May we use your comments in upcoming communications?   ____Yes   ____No

Please **FAX** this completed form to **888-991-5755**, or mail it to

Customer Service, Walch Publishing, P. O. Box 658, Portland, ME 04104-0658

We will send you a **FREE GIFT** in appreciation of your feedback. **THANK YOU!**